Animals

Ranger Rick

That Make Me Say

Ewww!

Animals Ranger Rick®
That Make Me Say
Ewww!

Dawn Cusick

imagine!
Publishing

An Imagine Book
Published by Charlesbridge
85 Main Street
Watertown, MA 02472
(617) 926-0329
www.charlesbridge.com

Library of Congress Cataloging-in-Publication Data
is available upon request.

ISBN: 978-1-62354-063-0

Printed in China. Manufactured in November, 2015.

(hc) 10 9 8 7 6 5 4 3 2 1

Display type and text type set in Motter Corpus and Frutiger.

Jacket and Type Design: Megan Kirby
Proofreading: Andrea McCarrick, Katy Nelson
Produced by EarlyLight Books

For information about custom editions, special sales,
premium and corporate purchases, please contact
Charlesbridge Publishing at specialsales@charlesbridge.com

Contents

African buffalo and oxpecker

Introduction

Welcome to a world that will make you say ewww!

We share Earth with millions of animals. Unlike our family pets, though, wild animals have to take care of themselves. The gross things they do are usually adaptations that help them survive.

Elephants and rhinos, for example, feed poop (also called feces) to their young so they will be able to digest plants. If the calves did not eat feces, they would starve to death. When gorillas and orangutans pick their noses and eat it, they aren't trying to gross us out. Instead, they are removing the dead skin and dried snot (called mucus) so they can smell food and nearby predators.

On your mark . . . get set . . . say ewww!

African
elephants

Cleanup
EWWW!

CLEANUP: Removing dirt, foreign matter, or pollution

Human cleanup is simple: we use toothpaste, soap, and shampoo. We clean ourselves to stay healthy and to make the people around us happy. Many animals clean themselves to stay healthy, too. They also clean up to find food and mates, or to help them escape predators. Get ready to say ewww!

gorilla

Food for Thought

Gorillas and chimpanzees often look at the stuff they remove from their noses before they—ewww!—eat it. There is so much competition for food in the wild that the small amount of energy in a booger is worth eating. Whoops—if you are reading this book at school, your teacher may prefer that you use the scientific word for booger: nasal detritus.

There's a Good Reason!

You can say ewww if you want to about nose picking, but for many animals, cleaning their noses may be important to their survival. Scent molecules move across wet surfaces easier than dry surfaces.

Gorillas, orangutans, and bonobos, and some other primates do not have outer nose surfaces that are wet, as bears and many other mammals do. Removing dried, crusty mucus from their noses helps gorillas and chimpanzees smell better. A better sense of smell helps them know when predators and good foods are nearby.

orangutan

gorillas

Cleanup EWWW!

Friend or Foe?

Having a bird beak in your nostril might seem like a huge ewww, but if you had a fly or other insect in your nose, that bird beak would be more like a woo-hoo than an ewww. Many large mammals in Africa spend a lot of time with several species (types) of birds. The birds get protection from some predators while feeding on high-protein insects, and the mammals get disease-causing insects removed from their bodies. They may also use cues from the birds as predator alarms. This type of relationship is called a symbiosis (sim-bye-O-sis).

African buffalo and oxpecker

Dinner-Napkin Tongue

Mammals often rub their tongues over their noses. (You're a mammal: How often do you clean your nose with your tongue?) These animals may be using their tongues like napkins, cleaning up leftover tidbits from dinner. It's also possible the animals are adding moisture to their noses, which can help them cool off and smell better.

dog

greater kudu antelope

Cleanup EWWW!

African elephant

Ponder This . . .

Elephants would need pretty long fingers to clean nasal detritus from their trunks! They clean their nostrils as they suck water in and spray it out.

Blow Your Nose

The exhaled air from a whale's blowhole is called a spout. Sometimes, a whale's spout can be seen from far away.

Not All Noses Can Be Cleaned

The blowholes in dolphins and other whales are nostril adaptations that usually do a good job of bringing oxygen to and carbon dioxide from their lungs. When oil spills pollute ocean waters, though, the oil can move through their blowholes and into their lungs. Oily lungs can cause breathing problems by making it harder for oxygen and carbon dioxide gases to move across lung tissue.

humpback whale

Cleanup EWWW!

Mud Baths Make Sense

How does rolling, splashing, and lounging in mud help keep animals clean? For mammals such as warthogs, rhinos, and elephants, which have little or no fur, mud helps protect their bodies from the sun's rays and cools them off. As the mud cakes, small skin parasites fall off.

warthog

white rhinoceroses

You Missed a Spot!

The wrinkly skin of elephants, rhinos, and hippos is an adaptation to hot habitats. The extra surface area these wrinkles provide helps the animals release more body heat. When mud gets in between the wrinkles in their skin, the mud's moisture can cool them off for many hours.

Asian elephant

African elephants

In a Pinch, Dust Will Do

When there's no mud nearby, elephants may spray themselves with dust for protection from the sun's rays. How do elephants keep from getting dust too far up their noses? Thousands of nerve cells tell their brains where the dust is, and their brains tell their nose muscles when to stop and start squeezing.

African elephant

Multi-Tasking Noses

An elephant's trunk is formed by adaptations to its upper lip and its nose. The trunk can be used like an extra arm for grasping, pulling, and lifting. Elephants also use their trunks for communication with other elephants; for guiding their young; and for spraying mud, water, and dust on themselves. An elephant's trunk has more than 150,000 groups of muscles!

Cleanup EWWW!

No Trunk? No Problem!

If you do not have a trunk, rolling on the ground in a dusty spot will get the job done. Many kinds of animals take dust baths to remove parasites or pieces of dead skin from their fur or feathers, including zebras, horses, rabbits, squirrels, swallows, quail, and some other birds.

ostrich

zebra

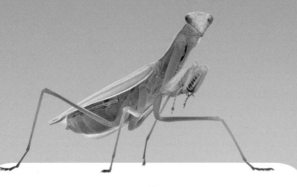

Every Last Bite?

The sharp spines on a praying mantis's front legs help it catch and hold food. Cleaning its spines helps it get every last bit of food energy. It also prevents bacteria and fungi from growing on the spines.

praying mantis

raccoon

Send Them to First Grade!

If a bear had a pine needle stuck in its toe, it might not notice. Raccoons would notice right away. Their feet are very sensitive, which helps them climb well and check out the quality of potential food. For raccoons, their teeth make good cleaning tools.

Cleanup **EWWW!**

Saliva Talks!

Mammal moms clean their offspring with saliva baths. Their saliva does more than clean and cool their young, though. Saliva has proteins in it that parents and littermates use to recognize each other.

lion

lions

First Bath

When a mammal mom cleans her offspring for the first time, she often needs to remove the sac that protected the newborn as it grew inside her. After birth, though, the sac needs to be removed quickly from the newborn's head to help it breathe.

bison

Cleanup **EWWW!**

pelican

Dirty Feathers Don't Work

Dirt and parasites can affect how well a bird's feathers work during flight, so most birds spend a lot of time preening, or cleaning their feathers. Birds have extra vertebrae in the neck area of their spinal cords, which helps them reach parts of their bodies you and I could never reach, even if we had long beaks!

golden mantled ground squirrel

Sun Bath

Many animals use sunlight to kill bacteria and other germs in their fur, feathers, and scales.

ravens

Getting to Know You . . . And Maybe Avoiding A Fight or Two

In some species of birds, cleaning the feathers around another bird's head is part of courtship. In other species, preening may prevent fights.

Social Grooming

Most primates spend a small amount of time grooming themselves and a lot of time grooming others. Biologists have noticed that when primates groom each other, their brains release extra chemicals that may help them form close bonds.

baboons

macaques

Cleanup EWWW!

Hold Still!

If you were hungry, would you climb inside a large predator's mouth to eat parasites from its teeth? Or swim near its open jaws to feed on parasites on its scales? You would if you were a cleaner shrimp or a cleaner wrasse! We could ask the eels a similar question: If you're hungry, why don't you eat the cleaner shrimp and fish that are oh-so-close to your mouth? The cleaners and the eels have a symbiotic relationship. Each one gains by behaving in these surprising ways. The cleaners get a meal, and the eels lose the parasites that can damage their health.

eel and wrasse

eel and cleaner shrimp

black bear

Recycling Ewww!

Hibernating grizzly and black bears do not urinate (pee) in their winter dens. Their bodies do make urea, the main ingredient in urine, as they burn their fat stores through the winter. Their bodies recycle nutrients from the urea to make proteins, which helps keep their muscles strong.

grizzly bear

Hold That Thought

Grizzly and black bears also do not defecate (poop) during hibernation. Their guts store the small amounts of waste their bodies produce until after they leave their dens.

Cleanup EWWW!

Perfect Pouch?

Marsupial pouches may seem like the perfect way to protect offspring. Animal adaptations are never perfect, though. Think about it for a minute: There's no toilet flush button in a kangaroo mom's pouch. Instead, she and other marsupial moms clean their pouches out with their tongues. Ewww!

red kangaroos

red fox kit

It's a Dirty Job . . .

Most mammal moms get their newborns to urinate and defecate by cleaning their bottoms. This may sound like a giant ewww to us, but what would happen if parents did not do this? The babies could develop life-threatening infections from bacteria and fungi that can grow in feces. Or, predators could use scent cues in feces and urine to find the babies.

chipmun

Cleanup EWWW!

tree swallow

Daily Chores for Birds, Too

Bird parents also need to remove their offspring's waste to keep their nests safe. Most newly hatched chicks expel gelatin-like packages called fecal sacs that contain body waste. For the first few weeks after their chicks hatch, parents remove these fecal sacs and waste-covered nest materials when they leave to find food.

cicada exoskeleton

Good News, Bad News

The exoskeletons of insects, spiders, crabs, and other arthropods provide protection from predators and the environment. Exoskeletons can cause problems for growing arthropods, though. In vertebrate animals, bones grow larger as the animals grow. In arthropods, their external skeletons do not grow with them. Instead, special hormones turn on genes for molting, causing arthropods to break out of their old exoskeletons and grow new ones.

cicada

cicada

Most arthropods are vulnerable after molting because their new exoskeletons take time to harden. Winged insects often molt while hanging upside down, which helps prevent their old exoskeletons from damaging their new wings.

Cleanup EWWW!

snake skin

Shedding Skin

Unlike arthropods, reptiles molt in several different ways. Turtles (above) molt in the scaly areas on their heads, necks, and limbs. Snakes (right and bottom) lose their outer scale layer (often called "skin") all at once. Lizards (below) molt all over their bodies but usually in small patches.

When? Why?

A reptile's outer scale layer does not grow with the rest of its body, so it molts when this outer layer no longer "fits." Reptiles that are growing a lot will molt more often than those that are not. Females often molt when their eggs mature and take up more space in their bodies.

white rhinoceroses

Dinner
EWWW!

DINNER: Food that animals ingest

Feces, vomit, carrion, and other gross things may make us say ewww!, but without using these as foods, many wild animals would die. Once digested, these foods give animals the same types of nutrients that pizza or chocolate cake would give us: proteins, sugars, and fats.

Sweet Treats?

How often do you say yum to honey? Even if you don't like eating honey on muffins or on a spoon straight from the jar, you are probably eating honey all the time. Many companies use it to sweeten desserts, breads, cereals, and drinks.

When you think about where honey comes from, you may say ewww for a minute or two. Honey bees make honey by vomiting (puking) the nectar they collect from flowers into compartments in their hives called cells. They also vomit chemicals into the cells, which helps turn the nectar into honey. In the winter, high-energy sugars in the honey provide food for the hive. In some cells, the honey also provides food for growing larvae.

honey bees

Dinner EWWW!

Plant Puzzles

Many plants make sweet nectar to attract pollinating animals. Plants usually make their pollinators work to get the nectar, though. While working to get the nectar, a yellow powder called pollen sticks to the pollinators. When the animals move to another flower, they carry the pollen with them. Plants use pollen that animals bring them from other plants to make fruit.

bumble bee

bumble bee

Prove It!

In some bird species, females do all of the chick care. In other species, both parents care for the eggs and feed the young. In these species, males often feed the females as part of courtship. This behavior is called courtship feeding. If males do not prove they can share food, females refuse to mate with them. Some research studies have shown that females lay more eggs when they get food from males.

Where do males get their courtship food? Not from grocery stores or restaurants! In species such as the common tern, males bring whole fish. In species such as the boobies, males puke up partly digested food for their mates.

common terns

Dinner EWWW!

Seeing Red

The insides of young bird mouths are usually red or orange. These bright colors signal their parents to bring them lots of food.

jays

robins

Do the Math

American robin parents can feed each of their chicks one hundred worms a day for two weeks! How many worms would robin parents need to raise a brood of four?

cardinals

Hungry Teenagers

Even though young cardinals leave their nests after just nine to ten days, their parents feed insects to them for almost two months.

Dinner **EWWW!**

great horned owl

Barfing Bones And Feathers

Birds of prey, such as owls, eagles, and hawks, have trouble digesting some materials from their prey. Their beaks may be very strong, but, like other birds, they do not have teeth for crushing their food.

A separate chamber in their stomachs, called the gizzard, stops bones and feathers from going into their main stomachs. They then throw up the parts they can't digest.

A Full Gizzard Can Mean Only One Thing!

Once a bird's gizzard fills up, the bird cannot eat again until the gizzard is emptied. The regurgitated gizzard material is called a pellet. When biologists and students dissect pellets, they find skeletons, fur, and feathers in there. Ewww!

pellet

burrowing owl

Beach Birds Barf, Too!

Birds that live near beaches, rivers, and lakes also regurgitate pellets from their gizzards. Their pellets contain fish bones.

Other pellet-puking birds include insectivores, which barf up insect exoskeletons, and frugivores, which barf up difficult-to-digest fruit seeds and skin.

black skimmer

African elephants

Dinner EWWW!

white rhinoceroses

bacteria

Healthy Eating

Eating feces would make humans sick. For several kinds of animals, though, eating feces is an important way to stay healthy. Rhinos (above) and elephants (left-hand page) eat feces to bring plant-digesting bacteria into their bodies. Young pandas, warthogs, and even termites also eat feces to get helpful bacteria inside them. Other animals, such as mice, eat feces as a way to get extra nutrition.

Carrion Carnivores

You can call it gross or you can call it cool, but many animals make a living eating rotting flesh, called carrion. Some animals eat only carrion, while others, such as crabs and sharks, eat carrion and freshly killed prey, depending on what they can find.

crab

blue shark

Dinner EWWW!

bald eagle

Tasty Treats?

Sharp, hooked beaks help carrion-eating birds, such as this bald eagle (above) and turkey vulture (right), tear through skin and fur. Uncooked, rotting flesh would smell and taste gross to us, but carrion-eating birds have different types of taste buds that are adapted to the foods they eat. They also use their sharp sense of smell to decide how old a carcass is. An old carcass releases more sulfur than a fresh one, and these birds prefer fresh carcasses.

Dinner EWWW!

Duck!

Skunks can aim their spray at a target several feet away. Their anal glands do not hold much spray, though, and it takes several days to make more, so they would rather threaten you than spray you.

Worse Than A Bite?

Most snakes have a defense that does not come from their mouths. Instead, it comes from musk glands near their tail. Snakes emit their bad-smelling musk when they feel threatened. Both venomous and non-venomous snakes use musk as a defense, and even small snakes can smell very bad.

skunk

Burning Spray

Chemicals in skunk spray can cause temporary blindness if they get in an animal's eyes.

garter snake

Last-Choice Chow

Foxes (above) and coyotes prey on skunks if they do not have other food choices. A face full of burning spray is worth it when you need energy.

great horned owl

Look Up!

Great horned owls and red-tailed hawks (above) are big skunk predators. Since these birds attack quickly from above, the skunks' spray defense does not help.

Chemistry Class

Skunk spray is made from seven types of molecules that produce the well-known bad-smelling yellow oil. Each skunk species' spray has a slightly different molecule recipe. The spray is made in two glands that empty into the anus.

leopard
and antelope

Protecting Your Prey

Leopards protect their large, freshly killed prey from carnivore thieves, such as hyenas and lions, by carrying it up trees. Smaller prey animals, such as rats and beetles, are eaten on the spot.

Dinner EWWW!

Protesting Prey

For bears that hibernate, it's important to eat enough food before winter for a healthy fat layer. For salmon, it's important to return to their spawning sites. A thrashing salmon is usually no match for a full-grown bear's teeth, but young bears may lose their grip, especially when trying to hold more than one fish.

black bear

Gotcha!

Most spiders and insects are no match for the strong grip and serrated spines of a praying mantis. Likewise, most mantises are no match for the sharp beaks and protective feathers of birds!

catbird and mantis

Atlantic puffin

Puffin Power!

Puffins use their strong bills and sharp edges on their tongues to hold many fish in their mouths at the same time. Their fish feasts happen in safe spots on the shore or back in their nests if they have chicks.

jumping spider

jumping spider

Good Thing We're Not Prey!

These jumping spiders might look cute, but there's nothing cute about the way they eat. Like other spiders, jumping spiders vomit up chemicals from their stomachs. The chemicals break down the sugars, proteins, and fats that make up their prey's bodies. Once the solid prey becomes a liquid, spiders drink it. Above and below: jumping spiders

Dinner EWWW!

Eating in Style

Most spiders inject poison into their prey, making them easier to eat. Other spiders wrap their prey tightly in a cocoon, crushing it. Then they vomit stomach chemicals on it so the food is easier to eat.

orb weaver

No Teeth? No Worries

Many insects, including roaches (above) and flies, also vomit up chemicals to help break down their food. Most other types of animals—even large animals with teeth—use chemicals to digest their food, too, but they have larger stomachs and larger intestines.

Dinner EWWW!

crab plovers

munias

Bug Buffet

It may look like a slimy mess to us, but many insects feed on the microscopic life that lives in and near algae, duckweed, and other water plants. For hungry birds, these feeding insects are an important part of their diet. These plants also provide camouflage for animals such as the turtles at far right.

night heron and raccoons

Take Another Look . . .

The camouflage and food sources that algae and aquatic plants provide may seem like a perfect part of stream and pond ecosystems, but they can cause big problems. Fish can be stressed by the low oxygen levels caused when algae and plants die and decay. The chemicals people use to kill algae and plants also damage important parts of food chains.

turtles

hippopotamuses

Encore
EWWW!

ENCORE: Something that is repeated again, often because the audience wants more

You may have said ewww a time or two as you've read through this book. Now, get ready for an encore. You'll find animals that use sticky spit, flying feces, toilet claws, squirting blood, scary vomit, sunscreen sweat, and more to help them compete in the natural world.

Wear a Raincoat to the Zoo?

What kind of dumbo throws poop at people in zoos? Smart chimpanzees do, that's who! Biologists compared chimps that threw feces and other objects well with chimps that threw less well. The results? The good throwers had more developed brains. Throwing objects at the right speed and in the right direction to hit a target takes more smarts than you might think.

Dr. Emily Weiss, who studies animal behavior, worked with poop-throwing chimps at a zoo for several years. Dr. Weiss says, "There is something about chimp poo . . . it is different from most poo (and trust me—I know my poo). The odor is extraordinary, and it has an oil in it that does not easily wash off. Simply said, you do not want to be hit with chimpanzee fecal matter." Keep Dr. Weiss's words in mind the next time you visit a zoo.

chimpanzees

Encore EWWW!

hippopotamuses

Is It a Bird? Is It a Plane?
Nope, It's Flying Hippo Dung!

Hippos move their flyswatter-like tails in fast circles when they poop, sending feces flying in many directions. Pooping this way lets them send their communication chemicals farther away. These chemicals mark their territories and tell other hippos who is boss.

The Feces Factor

Most humans are grossed out by the look and smell of poop, and many scientists believe these responses are adaptations that protect us from diseases.

In the natural world, poop plays many important roles in healthy ecosystems. Poop adds carbon, nitrogen, and other elements back into the environment. Poop also serves as food for many species of invertebrate animals, bacteria, and fungi.

Poop Pesticide

Ground-nesting birds such as blue-footed boobies and penguins protect their eggs from insects by spraying a circle of poop around their nests. How do they make such perfect circles? They stand in the middle of their nests, lift their tail feathers, and spray feces as they slowly turn all the way around.

blue-footed booby

flies

Fly Frenzy

Why are flies and other insects so attracted to feces? For some insects, poop is a fantastic food source. For others, it's a safe place to lay their eggs and has an added benefit: When their eggs hatch, dinner is waiting for their young.

How Long Can You Hold It?

Two-toed sloths avoid ground predators by defecating from high up in trees. Three-toed sloths do not poop from their tree homes. Instead, they climb down once a week, dig a hole, and poop in the ground.

Biologists believe the three-toed sloths come down to poop because it helps the moths and algae that use the sloths' fur for habitat. Female moths lay their eggs in the fresh sloth poop and then return to the trees in the sloths' fur. After the eggs hatch and become adults, the young moths fly upward to find a sloth to live with. Feces from the moths help to fertilize the algae. The algae add a green color to the sloths' fur, helping the sloths blend in with the trees they live in. Sloths eat some of the algae to get extra nutrients. Biologists still have a lot to learn about these symbiotic relationships. Maybe you will become a biologist and help them figure it out!

two-toed sloth

Encore EWWW!

Toilet Claws Instead of Toilet Paper

Small primates called tarsiers use two back toes on each foot to groom their fur, including the fur around their bottoms that can get feces tangled in it. These toes have claws on them. The rest of their toes and all of their fingers are flat with soft pads on them. The pads help tarsiers hang on to tree limbs and branches, both upside down and right-side up.

Chemical Conversations

If you asked a biologist why wild male goats smell so bad, he or she would say that male goats urinate on themselves to attract females with special chemicals in their urine. If you asked a third grader why male goats smell so bad, he or she might say, "Because they pee on themselves!" Male goats urinate on their chests, chins, abdomens, and foreheads. The urine tells females the age and health of the males. Both male and female deer urinate on their legs and feet to talk to each other with scent molecules.

Encore EWWW!

Wash Your Face!

Male capuchin monkeys and some other New World primates make people say ewww when they urinate in their cupped hands and then splash the urine over their faces and bodies.

Why would male capuchins do this? People used to think that males were using their urine to cool themselves off in hot weather, the way cats and other animals dampen their fur with saliva when they groom themselves. That idea, however, didn't explain why females don't wash themselves with urine.

Biologists now think males use chemicals in their urine to share information with females. Using a type of MRI test on capuchin brains, biologists discovered that when females smelled male urine, six different parts of their brains lit up.

capuchin

coyote

Stinky Tricks

Can you really buy animal urine with your allowance? Yes, you can, but why would you want to spend your hard-earned money that way? People sell urine from predators such as coyotes and foxes to ward off deer, rabbits, and browsing animals that can damage gardens.

Do a pH Test on This Spit!

Many animals vomit when they feel stress, either to startle predators or as part of their fight-or-flight response. When camels feel stress, small amounts of vomit bubble up from their stomachs, making a drippy, frothy mess around their mouths. Be sure to hit the ground fast if you see camel vomit headed your way. If you can't move away fast enough, make sure you shower soon, because camel spit-up really stinks!

Bactrian camels

Encore EWWW!

Lots & Lots of Sticky Spit

The long tube that moves food from the mouth to the stomach (called the esophagus) is extra long in giraffes because of their long necks. To help moisten their food for their long journeys, they produce lots of saliva when they are feeding. Giraffes also have very sticky saliva that protects their mouths and esophagi from sharp thorns on the twigs that hold the leaves they eat.

giraffes

short-horned lizard

Blood Squirt Attack

Many types of short-horned lizards inflate their spiny bodies to discourage predators. Some species also have a unique defense. They can squirt blood from sacs near their eyes at predators up to three feet away. The blood has chemicals in it that repel some large mammals such as wolves, coyotes, and dogs. Biologists believe these toxic chemicals may come from poisonous ants the lizards feed on.

hippopotamus

Blood Sweat Saves the Day

Ever wonder why some hippopotamuses look red or pink? People used to think that hippos were sweating blood, and they called the red liquid "blood sweat." Chemistry tests told a different story. Hippos do not have sweat glands to help keep them cool. Instead, they release a reddish-brown mucus that keeps their bodies moist. Some chemicals in the mucus work like sunscreen, protecting their skin from the sun's rays. Other chemicals in the liquid protect the hippos from bacteria.

frog

Breathe Easy

Amphibians such as frogs and salamanders have small lungs compared to most other vertebrates. A layer of mucus all over their skin helps oxygen move into their bodies and carbon dioxide move out. Earthworms do not have any lungs at all. They also use mucus to move gases in and out of their bodies.

Mucus Soap for Mother's Day?

Many animals, including earthworms (top right), secrete antibiotic chemicals in their mucus that kill bacteria. If these antibiotics work so well to kill bacteria, maybe biologists will learn to make human soaps or medicines with them. Animals such as these salamanders also secrete bad-tasting chemicals and toxins in their mucus, which helps protect them from predators.

salamander

salamander

Mucus Protects Turtle Embryos

Female sea turtles return to land, often after long migrations, to lay their eggs on shorelines. Females dig nest chambers with their flippers and then lay their eggs in the nests. They cover their eggs with mucus and sand. The mucus helps keep the eggs moist, and may protect them from bacteria and fungi.

Encore EWWW!

Salty, Mucus Tears?

Biologists have found special glands that help remove salt in marine turtles, desert tortoises, and even turtles that live on the Nile River. These glands, found in the corners of their eyes, are adaptations to tear glands. For sea turtles, these glands help their bodies remove extra salt that comes from drinking and living in salt water. For turtles in dry environments, the glands let them remove extra salt. When people see marine turtles releasing salt in mucus, it can look as though the turtles were crying!

sea turtle

More Salt Glands

Sea snakes and marine crocodiles have salt glands on their tongues. These glands keep the salt levels in their bodies from becoming too high. Marine birds such as the gull at right also have salt glands near their eyes. Their salty liquid leaves their bodies through nostrils on their bills.

crocodile

sea snake

Play Ball!

What's the mystery behind the hundreds of mud balls you might find along some shorelines? Do fiddler crabs play a lot of dodge ball? Or do they use them to camouflage their bodies or their burrows? Biologists used to believe crabs ejected the balls as they were digging their burrows. After more studying, they learned there are two types of mud balls. Some mud balls (usually the larger ones) are made when the crabs dig their burrows, while the smaller ones are made when crabs feed in the mud.

fiddler crab

African
hornbill

Trick Predators with Mud, Feces, and Fruit

Animals have some amazing ways to protect themselves from predators, but these African hornbills may take the prize. To prepare their nest, a mated pair searches for a natural opening in a tree. The female seals up most of the opening with mud.

Next, she goes inside and closes up all but a very small opening from the inside with a mixture of feces, mud, and sticky fruit. The male passes fresh-caught insects through to the female while she incubates the eggs and cares for the hatchlings. When the young birds need more food than the male can find by himself, the female breaks through part of the wall and starts helping her partner bring food to their offspring.

blister beetle

Blister Blood Fights off Predators (and Warts)

Can one small beetle make a large animal sick or blister the skin of a full-grown human? Yes, it can! Blister beetles defend themselves with reflex bleeding. When threatened, these beetles release drops of blood (called hemolymph) from their leg joints. This defense works because a chemical in their blood causes sickness and blisters in the animals they're defending themselves against. Females protect their developing offspring by adding a layer of this chemical to the outside of their eggs. Humans have used this chemical in some wart medicines.

Encore EWWW!

io caterpillar

monarch caterpillar

grasshopper

Stand Back, Jack!

Some caterpillars, grasshoppers, and other insects puke when a predator gets too close. This type of protection is called defensive regurgitation. The vomit surprises predators. It also may contain chemicals that make the insects taste bad to birds or that irritate small-er animals such as spiders and other insects.

Caterpillars use other types of defense, too. The io moth caterpillar (top left) use venomous spines for defense. Monarch caterpillars (top right) use toxins they get from the milkweed plants they eat for protection.

SCAVENGER HUNT CHALLENGES

Have you ever wondered how a caterpillar changes body form inside its chrysalis? First, the caterpillar releases special chemicals that turn most of its body into a kind of soup. Next, molecules in the soup reform to build an adult body with wings. **SCAVENGER HUNT CHALLENGE:** Search the Internet for chrysalis images. How many different chrysalis shapes can you find?

monarch chrysalis

mud dauber wasp

monarch caterpillar

The mud dauber wasp visits muddy areas to collect mud for its nest. It carries the mud back to its building sites with its front legs and then shapes the mud with its mouth and legs. **SCAVENGER HUNT CHALLENGES:** Inside, do an image search for "animals that make nests from mud." Find at least three kinds of animals that use mud to make nests. Outside, sit quietly near some mud. How many animals do you see there in half an hour? Remember, insects and spiders are animals, too!

SCAVENGER HUNT CHALLENGES

Look inside this tricolor heron's mouth. Do you see any teeth? Like all birds, herons do not have teeth because they evolved beaks to catch and kill their prey. **SCAVENGER HUNT CHALLENGES:** Inside, do an information search for "how birds digest food." Outside, find at least five types of birds and compare their bills.

tricolor heron

macaque

In India, macaques are protected and often live in special Hindu worship places called monkey temples. Tourists from all over the world visit the monkey temples. Some tourists behave badly, feeding human food to the monkeys and pulling their tails. The monkeys have become very comfortable around humans, and there are many reports of monkeys biting and scratching people. Sometimes the macaques surprise tourists by getting on their shoulders and urinating or defecating. Ewww! **SCAVENGER HUNT CHALLENGE:** Inside, do an information search for "how to behave near a wild animal."

READ MORE

FROM THE NATIONAL WILDLIFE FEDERATION:

FUN ON THE WEB:
nwf.org/Kids for a world of kids' fun

MAGAZINES:

OTHER BOOKS IN THE SERIES:

ANIMALS THAT MAKE ME SAY WOW! by Dawn Cusick;
    Imagine/Charlesbridge (2014).

ANIMALS THAT MAKE ME SAY OUCH! by Dawn Cusick;
    Imagine/Charlesbridge (2014).

OTHER BOOKS FROM THE AUTHOR:

GET THE SCOOP ON ANIMAL PUKE!;
    Imagine/Charlesbridge (2014).

GET THE SCOOP ON ANIMAL POOP!;
    Imagine/Charlesbridge (2012).

ANIMAL SNACKS;
    EarlyLight Books (2012).

ANIMAL EGGS;
    EarlyLight Books (2012).

COOL ANIMAL NAMES;
    Imagine/Charlesbridge (2011).

Adaptation: A change in an organism's behavior or form that helps it compete better.

Behavior: The ways organisms act.

Carnivore: An animal that eats other animals.

Communication: The sharing of information. Some organisms communicate with sounds or movements, while others communicate with colors or chemicals.

Diffusion: The movement of gasses or liquids from places of higher concentration to places of lower concentration.

Ecosystem: The living and nonliving parts of an environment functioning together.

Habitat: The home for an organism or a group of organisms.

Herbivore: An animal that eats plants.

Parasite: An organism that uses other organisms for food and habitat.

Predator: An organism that preys on other organisms.

Prey: An animal being hunted or eaten by another animal.

Regurgitate: To vomit partially digested food.

Territory: An area that an organism lives in and defends.

Toxin: A poisonous substance produced by organisms to help defend themselves from predators or to help them kill prey.

Venom: Poison used by an organism as part of its defense or to find food that is moved through a bite or a sting.

African buffalo

Stinky sniffing? Animals such as this African buffalo get information about other animals with their sense of smell.

RESEARCH

The author would like to thank and acknowledge the following scientists, organizations, and institutions for their research assistance.

From the National Wildlife Federation:

Mary Dalheim, Kathy Kranking, Ellen Lambeth, Hannah Schardt, Deana Duffek, Michael Morris, the entire Ranger Rick publication staff, and NWF Naturalist David Mizejewski

From Other Sources:

Arizona Museum of Natural History, Leslie S. Babonis, J. A. Bagget, Boyce Thompson Arboretum in Arizona, C.D. Brand, François Brischoux, Bronx Zoo Wildlife Conservation Society, G. Brown, C.A. Buzzell, Charles Darwin Research Station, Cincinnati Zoo, William E. Cooper, Cornell Lab of Ornithology/All About Birds, David S. Dobkin, R.I.M. Dunbar, Paul R. Ehrlich, Thomas R. Fasulo, Dennis M. Ferraro, Dale Fishbeck, Jennifer E. Frick, J.B. Grant, K.A. Gunther, S. Halkin, M.A. Haroldson, Thomas L. Harrison, David C. Hartnett, N. Holder, William D. Hopkins, International Union for Conservation of Nature, Ferris Jabr, Joan S. Jeffrey, Melissa Kaplan, Peter Kingsley-Smith, Rebecca Kreston, S. Linville, Rebecca A. Martusewicz, Colleen McCann, E. Moreau, National Marine Center, New England Aquarium, Knut Schmidt-Nielsen, North Carolina Wildlife Resources Commission, R. Nowak, Ohio Division of Wildlife, National Park Service, J. Paradiso, Jonathan Pauli, PBS Nature, Kenneth E. Petit, K.A. Phillips, Primate Behavior Research Group/Harvard University, Ranger Rick Magazine, Paul A. Rees, Clifford G. Rice, Joshua Rottman, Jamie L. Russell, Yoko Saikawa, Saylor Foundation, Jennifer A. Schaeffer, C.C. Schwartz, Sea Turtle Conservancy, Aurora Sebastiani, Richard B. Selander, Wade C. Sherbrooke, C.C. Sherwood, O. Soave, South Carolina Department of Natural Resources, South Dakota Game, Fish and Parks, John H. Sparks, M.A. Ternent, C.H. Vanderwolf, Stephen Vantassel, Washington Department of Fish and Wildlife, Emily Weiss, Elizabeth Wenner, Darryl Wheye, Paul Wolterbeek, William F. Wood, and Rachel Wright

PHOTO CREDITS

The author would like to thank the following photographers for their creative contributions.

From the National Wildlife Federation Photography Archives:

From Shutterstock:

INDEX